O'Brien

HARRY S. TRUMAN

No other president has been so out-spoken in his opinions and judgments of men and events that shaped American history. The people loved Truman for his candid, no-nonsense comments. They would yell, "Give 'em hell, Harry!" But Truman's answer was, "I never give them hell. I just tell the truth and they think it is hell."

GIVE 'EM HELL, HARRY!

Edited by Mark Goodman

AWARD BOOKS
NEW YORK

FIRST AWARD PRINTING 1974

CONTENTS

"Always do right. This will gratify some people and astonish the rest."

—Mark Twain

The Buck Stops Here

Signs on President Truman's desk at the White House.

SENATOR TRUMAN

As a newly elected Senator, Truman made a quick visit to Washington. When he returned to Missouri, he was greeted by local reporters.

"I'll do my best and keep my feet on the ground. That's one of the hardest things for a Senator to do, it seems. All this precedence and other hooey accorded a Senator isn't very good for the Republic.

"The association with dressed-up diplomats has turned the head of more than one Senator I can tell you. My trouble is that I probably won't find a place to live. You see, I have to live on my salary, and a cubbyhole rents for a hundred and fifty dollars a month there. The ones that are fit to live in run from two hundred and fifty to five hundred a month and although it's hard to believe, there are some saphead Senators who pay fifteen hundred dollars a month for their apartments."

November, 1934

Harry Truman: "I would like very much to have a chance to work in this war as a field artillery colonel."
General Marshall: "Senator, how old are you?"
Truman: "Well, I'm fifty-six."
Marshall: "You're too damned old. You'd better stay home and work in the Senate."
Truman: "You're three years older than I am."
Marshall: "I know, but I'm already a general."

1940

I'm content just where I am. I'm happy in the Senate. I have friends and I don't have any political ambitions. You know, people call me a politican, and you know the way some say it. Well, you've got to be a politician in the first place to get to be a Senator. When you're dead, they call you a statesman . . .

Addressing the Representatives of Management and Labor at a meeting in Philadelphia, Truman remarked:

"I can't let Jim Wadsworth have you believe that he is the only farmer in the place. I am one, too. And there are a great many people who would tell you that that is still where I belong."

November 19, 1943

Harry Truman was once asked whether he might consider running for Vice-President:

"I don't want to be Vice-President. I bet I can go down on the street and stop the first ten men I see, and that they can't tell me the names of two of the last ten Vice-Presidents of the United States."

In 1944 Truman was mentioned as a possible Vice-Presidential candidate. When he was told that F.D.R. would endorse him for the nomination, Truman replied, "Tell him to go to hell. I'm for Jimmy Byrnes."

In rebutting an attack made on Secretary of State Dean Acheson, Truman said, "How our position in the world would be improved by the retirement of Dean Acheson from public life is beyond me. Mr. Acheson has helped shape and carry out our policy of resistance to communist imperialism . . . If communism were to prevail in the world—as it shall not prevail—Dean Acheson would be one of the first, if not the first to be shot by the enemies of liberty."

1944

THE PRESIDENTIAL YEARS

When Truman became President after the death of Franklin Delano Roosevelt, he remarked:

"Did you ever have a bull or a load of hay fall on you? If you have, you know how I felt last night. I felt as if two planets and the whole constellation had fallen on me. I don't know if you boys pray, but if you do, please pray to God to help me carry this load."

⟨⟩

Aggressors cannot dominate the human mind. As long as hope remains, the spirit of man will never be crushed.

April 16, 1945

⟨⟩

In recent years, our enemies have clearly demonstrated the disaster which follows when freedom of thought is no longer tolerated. Honest minds cannot long be regimented without protest.

April 25, 1945

~~~

For years to come the success of our efforts
for a just and lasting peace will depend upon
the strength of those who are determined to
maintain that peace. We intend to use all our
moral influence and all our physical strength to
work for that kind of peace. We can ensure such
a peace only so long as we remain strong. We
must face the fact that peace must be built upon
power as well as upon good will and good deeds.

Address, Joint Session of Congress
October 23, 1945

~~~

Cooperation in peacetime is a hard thing to
get. There is no incentive to cooperate like there
is in war. Bring anybody here during wartime
and you get results from him—he was glad to
help the government. Now they are all trying
to help themselves, and it's just as hard as hell
for the President to get any help.

April 18, 1946

Wars are different from baseball games where, at the end of the game, the teams get dressed and leave the park.

April, 1946

There is at least one defense against the atomic bomb. That defense lies in our mastering this science of human relationships all over the world. It is the defense of tolerance and of understanding, of intelligence and thoughtfulness.

May 11, 1946

Sometimes the struggle for something that is worthwhile makes it all the better, after you get it.

Remarks, Conference on Education
July 11, 1946

❦

REPORTER: "In that connection, sir, do you want to run in 1948?"

PRESIDENT TRUMAN: "I am not thinking of 1948 now. I am trying to get through 1946."

❦

The plain people of this country found the courage and the strength, the self-discipline, and the mutual respect to fight and to win, with the help of our allies, under God. I doubt if the tasks of the future are more difficult. But if they are, then I say that our strength and our knowledge and our understanding will be equal to those tasks.

January 21, 1946

❦

All the questions which now beset us in strikes and wages and working conditions would be so much simpler if men and women were willing to apply the principles of the Golden Rule—"Do as you would be done by." And "Consider the beam in your eye and pay less attention to the mote in your brother's."

March 6, 1946

If the civilized world as we know it today is to survive, the gigantic power which man has acquired through atomic energy must be matched by spiritual strength of greater magnitude. All mankind now stands in the doorway to destruction—or upon the threshold of the greatest age in history. Only a high moral standard can master this new power of the universe, and develop it for the common good.

March 6, 1946

After he had fired Henry Wallace as Secretary of Commerce, Truman wrote to his mother:

"Well, I had to fire Henry today and, of course, I hated to do it. If Henry had stayed as Secretary of Agriculture in 1940 as he should have, there'd never have been all the controversy and I would not be here, and wouldn't that be nice? Charlie Ross said I'd rather be right than President and I told him I'd rather be anything than President.

"Well, now he's out, and the crackpots are having conniption fits. I'm glad they are. It convinces me I'm right."

September, 1946

On Henry Wallace: "Aeschives is the person Henry most resembles. Of course, when Alcibiades went over to the enemy, that is Sparta, he followed a life that Henry is now following. It is a most difficult thing these days to find reporters and editors who know anything about Ancient History."

Truman gave his opinion on Drew Pearson in a letter to Bob Hannigan concerning Pearson's broadcast "which gave the impression that he would not support Truman in 1948." Truman said: "Articles like that are merely an attempt to upset the "apple cart" and Pearson and your friend Winchell are the "Sphere heads" for that purpose. If either one of them ever tells the truth, it is by accident, and not intentional."

Sept. 10, 1946

Great republics of the past always passed away when their peoples became prosperous and fat and lazy, and were not willing to assume their responsibilities.

December 20, 1946

We have found it is easier for men to die together on the field of battle than it is for them to live together at home in peace.

December 24, 1946

When Truman was visiting Mexico, Mexican President Aleman asked him what he thought of the Paricutin volcano, the world's youngest mountain, which had erupted into birth only four years earlier.

"Frankly," Truman replied, "it's nothing compared to the one I'm sitting on in Washington."

March, 1947

One of the great lessons of history is that no nation can be stronger than its agriculture. Hungry and ill-nourished people cannot practice the art of democratic government and peaceful commerce. Peace cannot be built on a foundation of human want.

June 7, 1947

Speaking before the Gridiron Club in Washing, D.C.:

"Glad to be here—it was a great show. You have given me a lot of hints which I know will be helpful to me.

"I would like to reciprocate by discussing with you the various techniques of those citizens who are anxious to sacrifice themselves upon the altar of public service and become host to the nation at 1600 Pennsylvania Avenue.

"The last time I was here I explained to a speaker one method which had been successfully pursued. I hope the explanation proved useful.

"Since then I have been observing the various methods pursued by other citizens, who seem to have other ideas on the subject—which I am sure would have a large sale among governors and senators.

"For instance, one of them is to get elected Governor of New York. The method has succeeded in the past. It may yet be a good formula. It has not always succeeded, but you remember that old copybook admonition, 'If at first you do not succeed, try, try again.'

"Platform and politics need not be any trouble—just adopt the Democratic platform and say you can do it better.

"Perhaps a nonpolitical trip around the country far, far in advance of the Convention might improve the chances of the aspirant.

"Then there is a senatorial approach. You might say that I used that myself. Get yourself elected from Ohio. One of the states known as the mother of Presidents.

"There is a third way being pursued in the Senate—there are dozens of methods being pursued in the Senate. Be shy and aloof, say you want to go home and write your memoirs. Say you would not touch the crown with a ten-foot pole—refuse it at least thrice—but say nothing about just taking it in hand and wearing it at the proper time. This method may bring home the bacon.

"There is another and an intriguing method known as the foreign-travel method. When following this method, heads of foreign states should be interviewed—particularly Uncle Joe —the Generalissimo's views should be carefully publicized. The stay-at-homes should be impressed by Stalin's love for them and it should be strongly emphasized how well Uncle Joe can talk—I repeat—talk cooperation. Who can say —it used to be from the log cabin to the White House. Now it may be from the Kremlin to the White House. You never can tell, it might work."

May, 1947

Truman wrote three whimsical memoranda while at the White House, just before Christmas, 1947.

"I have appointed a Secretary of Semantics —a most important post. He is to furnish me forty to fifty dollar words. Tell me how to say yes and no in the same sentence without a contradiction. He is to tell me the combination of words that will put me against inflation in San Francisco and for it in New York. He is to show me how to keep silent—and say everything. You can very well see how he can save me an immense amount of worry."

"Then I have appointed a Secretary of Reaction. I want him to abolish flying machines and tell me how to restore ox-carts, oar boats, and sailing ships. What a load he can take off my mind if he will put the atom back together so it cannot be broken up. What a worry that will abolish for both me and Vyshinsky."

"I have appointed a Secretary for Columnists. His duties are to listen to all radio commentators, read all columnists in the newspaper from ivory tower to lowest gossip, coordinate them and give me the result so I can run the United States and the world as it should be. I have several able men in reserve besides the present holder of the job, because I think in a week or two, the present Secretary for Columnists will need the services of a psychiatrist and will in all probability end up in St. Elizabeth's."

❧

Just keep up the good work. I am perfectly willing to turn the country over to you when your time comes.

> Speaking to a group of young people,
> August 31, 1947

❧

The moral force of women has always had a wholesome influence upon the character of our civilization. They are deeply responsive to the fundamental human values. Women care more for people than for dollars, more for healthy children than fat dividends. Women want a society in which we build schools instead of prisons. Women want a world in which we sow and harvest the seeds of a good life instead of the seeds of war.

> October 8, 1947

There are a great many instances where editorials are mailed to me from out of town . . . I get up before daylight every morning—I have the reveille habit—and I spend a good part of that time going over all the Washington papers and the New York papers, *Baltimore Sun, Philadelphia Bulletin,* and many others that I have time to read. But I read them myself because I like to read them.

And I find out lots of things about myself that I never heard of.

October 17, 1947

For conservation of the human spirit, we need places such as Everglades National Park where we may be more keenly aware of our Creator's infinitely varied, infinitely beautiful, and infinitely bountiful handiwork. Here we may draw strength and peace of mind from our surroundings. Here we can truly understand what that great Israelitist Psalmist meant when he sang: "He maketh me to lie down in green pastures, He leadeth me beside still waters; He restoreth my soul."

. . . Conservation has been practiced for many decades and preached for many more, yet only in recent years has it become plain that we cannot afford to conserve in a haphazard or piecemeal manner. No part of our conservation program can be slighted if we want to make full use of our resources and have full protection against future emergencies.

December 6, 1947

⤛⤜

The basic source of our strength is spiritual. For we are a people with a faith. We believe in the dignity of man. We believe that he was created in the image of the Father of us all. We do not believe that men exist merely to strengthen the state or to be cogs in the economic machine. We do believe that governments are created to serve the people and that economic systems exist to minister to their wants. We have a profound devotion to the welfare and rights of the individual as a human being.

Annual Message to Congress on the
State of the Union
January 7, 1948

These men who live in the past remind me
of a toy I'm sure all of you have seen. The toy
is a small wooden bird called the Floogie Bird.
Around the Floogie Bird's neck is a label
reading: "I fly backwards. I don't care where
I'm going. I just want to see where I've been."

These backward-looking men refuse to see
where courageous leadership can take this
Nation in the years that lie ahead. These men
of small vision and faint hearts have set up
their familiar cry, "Of course it's fine, but it
can't be done."

How history repeats itself! How familiar all
this must sound to those who study the story
of Jefferson's Louisiana Purchase, or Jackson's
efforts to open up the West!

The men who ridiculed Jefferson and Jackson
were men of small courage and big fears. Their
political descendants are to be found among
those who were afraid to attempt recovery in
the 1930s and who are now afraid to make
farsighted preparations for American prosperity.

February 19, 1948

I am amazed, sometimes, when I find that some of you disagree with me. When I consider how you disagree among yourselves, I am somewhat comforted. I begin to think that maybe I'm all right, after all!

Address, American Society of
Newspaper Editors
April 17, 1948

I have just been reading a book by a fellow named Pollard—*Presidents and the Press!*
When you read what the press had to say about Washington, Jefferson, and Lincoln, and the other Presidents, you would think that we never had a decent man in the office since the country began.

April 23, 1948

I invited Stalin to come to Washington, and he said, "God willing, I will come." Well, I haven't met anybody yet who believes me, but that is what he said to me.

April 23, 1948

The life expectancy of the human man in Caesar's time was thirty-one years. It is now over sixty—I think sixty-two. If we keep that up, we will all be so old that we will join the Townsend Plan and be paying taxes to keep each other in pensions so we can live forever.

May 1, 1948

Children and dogs are as necessary to the welfare of this country as Wall Street and the railroads.

May 6, 1948

You cannot stamp out communism by driving it underground. You can prevent communism by more and better democracy.
    . . . You cannot stop the spread of an idea by passing a law against it.

June 4, 1948

The ideas of requiring Communist organizations to divulge information about themselves is a simple and attractive one. But it is about as practical as requiring thieves to register with the sheriff.

In earlier years I came to Chicago on shopping trips with Mrs. Truman. I enjoyed looking in the windows. No one paid any attention to me then. I suppose a lot of people wish I was looking in the windows again. But they won't get their way because a year from now I'm going to be right back in the same trouble I'm in now.

June, 1948

To reporters in Washington as he was leaving on a cross country "nonpolitical" whistle-stop train trip: "If I felt any better I couldn't stand it."

June, 1948

You know that education is one thing that can't be taken away from you. Nobody can rob you of your education, because that is in your head; that is, if you have any head and are capable of holding it. Most of us are capable of holding an education, if we try to get it.

June 11, 1948

I have a little hesitation about addressing this august body, shall I say, everybody with degree emeritus and all the other $40 words that go with an education. The only degree that I ever earned was at George Washington University in Washington, D.C. My daughter went to school there for four years and earned me a degree.

University of California
June 12, 1948

I think you're entitled to see your President
and to understand what his policies are and
what he is thinking about. It wouldn't make
any difference where I went, on what excuse
I went, or what I did. It's a political matter so
far as the Government of the United States is
concerned. The President can't cross the street
without creating an incident. But this President likes to create incidents.

June 12, 1948

I believe that atomic energy should not be
used to fatten the profits of big business. I
believe that it should be used to benefit all the
people. The largest private corporation in the
world is far too small to be entrusted with such
power, least of all for its own profit.

October 14, 1948

〜〜〜

  As President of the United States, I had the
fateful responsibility of deciding whether or
not to use the atom bomb for the first time. It
was the hardest decision I ever had to make.
But the President cannot duck hard problems
—he cannot pass the buck. I made the decision
after discussions with the ablest men in our
government, and after long and prayerful
consideration. I decided that the bomb should
be used in order to end the war quickly and
save countless lives—Japanese as well as American. But I resolved then and there to do
everything I could to see that this awesome
discovery was turned into a force for peace and
the advancement of mankind. Since then, it
has been my constant aim to prevent its use
for war and to hasten its use for peace.

                                October 14, 1948

The Constitution declares that there shall
be no "titles" of nobility in this Republic. It
does not say that there shall be no nobility. We
do have what may be described with exact
justice as a nobility. But it is not attained by
birth. One may come to it from a camp, as
Jackson did, or from a university, as Polk did,
or from a tailor's bench, as Johnson did. The
test is long and brave and honest labor for the
country's good.

October 19, 1948

While taking a post-election rest at the Key
West submarine base, President Truman allowed a gray stubble to grow on his chin.
Encountering Truman at the officers' pool, a
newsman remarked, "Mr. President, it looks
like you're growing a Vandyke."

The President answered, "That not a Vandyke, that's a Jeff Davis."

November 22, 1948

I had my sandwich and glass of buttermilk and went to bed at six-thirty. And along about twelve o'clock, I happened to wake up for some reason or other, and the radio was turned on to the National Broadcasting Company. And Mr. Kaltenborn and Mr. Harkness were reporting the situation as it then developed.

Mr. Kaltenborn was saying, "While the President is a million votes ahead of the popular vote, when the country vote comes in Mr. Truman will be defeated by an overwhelming majority."

Mr. Harkness came on, and analyzed the situation as it was then, and as Mr. Kaltenborn had recorded it. And to the sorrow of myself, and to those who were listening with me, it looked very much as if the election would be thrown into the House of Representatives because, of course, it was not possible for me to get a majority of the electoral votes. I went back to bed, and went to sleep.

About four o'clock in the morning, the Chief of the Secret Service came in and said, "Mr. President, I think you had better get up and listen to the broadcast. We have been listening all night."

And I said, "All right." I turned the darn thing on, and there was Mr. Kaltenborn again. Mr. Kaltenborn was saying, "While the President has a lead of two million votes, it is certainly necessary that this election shall go into the House of Representatives. He hasn't an opportunity of being elected by a majority of the electoral votes of the Nation!"

And Mr. Harkness came on and analyzed the situation.

I called the Secret Service men in, and I said, "We'd better go back to Kansas City, it looks as if I'm elected!"

Along about ten o'clock, I had a telegram which said that the election was over, and that I should be congratulated on the fact that I had won the election. Apparently it was too bad, but it happened!

Remarks, Dinner of Presidential
Electors
January 19, 1949

CRWC

Mr. Truman had invited the men from his old Battery D to march in his inaugural parade, saying he himself wouldn't be able to march along with them. "I'll be wearing a high silk hat and a long-tailed coat and I'm not going to march along in that rig."

January 31, 1949

CRWC

At the end of the 1949 Inaugural parties, the exhausted President Truman remarked:
"It's been a wonderful day. But I'm glad it comes only once every four years."

CRWC

After speaking to a group of college students about honesty, President Truman presented each student with a pen which was inscribed: "I swiped this from Harry S. Truman."

February, 1949

There isn't a word in the English language that has been so severely abused during the last ten years as the word democracy.

March 20, 1949

There was an old county judge who was with me on the county court in Jackson County, who was a nephew of Senator Money from Mississippi, who had been here in Washington with Senator Money, and who was a very great philosopher. And he gave me some advice before I left Independence to come to Washington. He said, "Harry, don't you go to the Senate with an inferiority complex. You sit there about six months, and you wonder how you got there. And after that you wonder how the rest of them got there."

April 6, 1949

REPORTER: "Your first four years will be up on the twelfth. Is there any comment you would like to make on your first four years as President?"

PRESIDENT TRUMAN: "I always say the first four years are the hardest."

> Press Conference
> April 7, 1949

I'm going to run again when I'm ninety. I've announced that a time or two, and you know, some damn fool looked the situation over and said, "When you're ninety, it's an off year," so I can't even run then. I didn't know I was going to stir up all that trouble.

> April 28, 1949

We don't propose, like some people, to meet today's problems by saying that they don't exist, and tomorrow's problems by wishing that tomorrow wouldn't come.

> September 29, 1949

෧෧෨

There is strength in a federation of any sort. We speak of a "helping hand." But a hand, just by itself, can't help anyone. It is dependent upon muscles, nerves, bloodstream, and brain, a federation of services, mutually helpful.

September 30, 1949

෧෧෨

I was a great admirer of old D.H. Burnham of Chicago, who organized the Chicago regional planning, and he had a motto over his mantel on which was written "MAKE NO LITTLE PLANS." You can always amend a big plan, but you never can expand a little one. I don't believe in little plans. I believe in plans big enough to meet a situation which we can't possibly foresee now.

November 2, 1949

The reactionaries hold that government policies should be designed for the special benefit of small groups of people who occupy positions of wealth and influence. Their theory seems to be that if these groups are prosperous, they will pass along some of their prosperity to the rest of us. This can be described as the "trickle down theory."

November 3, 1949

I am particularly anxious that we should do everything within our power to protect the minds and hearts of our children from the moral corruption that accompanies organized crime. Our children are our greatest resource, and our greatest asset—the hope of our future, and the future of the world. We must not permit the existence of conditions which cause our children to believe that crime is inevitable and normal. We must teach idealism—honor, ethics, decency, the moral law. We must teach that we should do right because it is right, and not in the hope of any material reward.

February 15, 1950

A politician is a man who understands government. Usually, if he understands it well enough and has made a reputation, as he should have, he will wind up—when he is dead—by being called a statesman. You have to have your own definition of what to call things political. It depends altogether on what your viewpoint is. If you are for it, it is statesmanlike. If you are against it, it is purely low politics!

February 23, 1950

There is too much nonsense about striped trousers in foreign affairs. Far more influence is exerted at home by the baggy pants of the managing editor than ever is exerted by the striped pants in the State Department.

April 20, 1950

It's the President's privilege to appoint generals—and sometimes to fire them when it's necessary. It's not a pleasant procedure at all. If you look through the history of the country, you'll find that James K. Polk had to do that; Abraham Lincoln had to do it four times, and one of the fellows—after Lincoln had fired him—ran against him for President. It didn't happen in my case!

April 27, 1950

About the meanest thing you can say about a man is that he means well.

May 10, 1950

Money spent for education is a valuable investment in the future of this country. We should move forward and secure a brighter future for the generations in the coming years that will guide the Nation. There is nothing that could be more important to our country's welfare.

May 12, 1950

Speaking at the White House to members of Ohio's Farm Bureau Federation, ex-farmer Truman said of his nephews Gilbert and Harry Truman (sons of his brother Vivian): ". . . these boys are good farmers and they have that sort of reputation. The only handicap they have is that their uncle is President of the United States. You know what a terrible handicap that is to a family."

June 5, 1950

If you tell Congress everything about the world situation, they get hysterical. If you tell them nothing they go fishing.

July 17, 1950

Referring to a bill he vetoed on the last possible day, although he had intended all along to veto it, Truman said he felt like the blacksmith on the jury out in Missouri when the judge asked him if he felt any prejudice against the defendant. "Oh, no, Judge, I think we should give him a fair trial, then I think we ought to take the s.o.b. out and string him up."

June 26, 1950

I pinned a medal on General MacArthur the other day, and told him I wished I had a medal like that, and he said that it was my duty to give medals, not to receive them. That is always the way. About all I receive are the bricks. It's a good thing I have got a pretty hard head, or it would have been broken a long time ago.

October 24, 1950

We cannot insulate our children from the
uncertainties of the world in which we live or
from the impact of the problems which con-
front us all. What we can do—and what we must
do—is to equip them to meet these problems, to
do their part in the total effort, and to build up
those inner resources of character which are
the main strength of the American people.

December 5, 1950

We are willing to negotiate differences, but
we will not yield to aggression. Appeasement
of evil is not the road to peace.

December 15, 1950

I have an old definition for a statesman, a
very old one: A statesman is a dead politician.

January 11, 1951

I want to express appreciation to this orchestra for rendering the things that I think most of, and I want to pay a compliment to that young Mr. Graham who sang here a while ago. He has a lovely voice, and I want to give him the same advice that I gave my daughter. He is seventeen years old. You finish that education and get yourself a degree from a standard college—I don't care which one it is—because nobody can take that away from you. Then, if you feel that you want a musical career, go and get it. That is what my baby did. I wouldn't let her start in the musical profession until she had finished her education at George Washington University, and she not only spent four years getting herself a degree, she got me one for nothing!

Remarks, Dinner in Honor of Joshua
Evans, Washington, D.C.
January 24, 1951

When things look difficult, there are always a lot of people who want to quit. We had people like that in the Revolutionary War, and we have had them in every war and every crisis of our history. Thomas Paine called them summer soldiers and sunshine patriots.

February 3, 1951

I've got other things to do besides watch television. I never look at it unless my daughter is on it.

March 29, 1951

My favorite animal is the mule. He has a lot more horse sense than a horse. He knows when to stop eating. And he knows when to stop working.

January, 1952

⚜

You cannot get along in the atomic age with horse-and-buggy ideas.

January 27, 1952

⚜

And what I want to say to historians is that any Monday morning quarterback can win a ball game next Monday, but he can't do it on Saturday.

April 27, 1952

⚜

Truman liked to quote his friend Harry Vaughan when asked why he wasn't running for the Presidency in 1952:

" 'If you don't like the heat, get out of the kitchen.' Well, that's what I'm doing."

Some of the generals and the admirals and the career men in government look upon the occupant of the White House as only a temporary nuisance who soon will be succeeded by another temporary occupant who won't find out what it is all about for a long time and then it will be too late to do anything about it.

1952

I have served my time . . . I don't want to be carried out of the White House in a pine box.

July 27, 1952

I like Ike—I like Ike so well I would send him back to the Army if I had a chance.

October 12, 1952

❧❦❧

I have done the best I could; the best for the people. I hope it was enough.

January 25, 1953

❧❦❧

While Mr. Truman was preparing to vacate the White House in January, 1953, he remarked:

"If I had known there would be so much work leaving this place, I'd have run again."

1948 PRESIDENTIAL CAMPAIGN

Visiting President Truman at the White House in September, 1948, a New York newspaper publisher asked, "By the way, Mr. President, what exactly made you decide to run [for a second term]?"

Looking around the room, Truman replied with a grin, "Where would I ever find another house like this?"

∽◦∾

That fact that we have had a Republican Congress for two years has at least given you a chance to see what they are like and what they will do. I call it the worst Congress, except one, this country has ever had. Because I was in the White House, however, they didn't get to walk backwards quite as fast as they wanted to.

September 6, 1948

Today too many Americans in country clubs and fashionable resorts are repeating, like parrots, the phrase "labor must be kept in its place." It is time that all Americans realized that the place of labor is side by side with the businessman and with the farmer, and not one degree lower.

September 6, 1948

It is time that every American recognize what our fathers knew—that it is an honorable thing to work with your hands.

September 6, 1948

It is a little too early in the morning to make a real political talk, or a non-political talk, because this is supposed to be a non-political trip. That all depends on your viewpoint. If you are on my side, it's non-political; if you are not, it's a low-down political trip, to come out and tell the people what they ought to hear.

∽✠∾

This year the same candidate is back with us, and he is saying much the same thing; that he likes our Democratic laws, but that he can run them better than we can.

It sounds like the same old phonograph record; but this year the record has a crack, and the needle gets stuck in it. The crack was provided by the Republican Eightieth Congress.

In 1948, every time the candidate says, "I can do it better," the crack says, "We're against it."

∽✠∾

REPORTER: "There was a report that you might make five hundred appearances between Labor Day and Election Day?"

PRESIDENT TRUMAN: "Well, as Mark Twain said about his death, I think that is rather exaggerated."

Press Conference
September 9, 1948

I can plow a straight furrow. A prejudiced witness said so—my mother.

National Plowing Contest campaign speech,
Dexter, Iowa
September 18, 1948

I heard a fellow tell a story about how he felt when he had to make speeches. He said when he has to make a speech, he felt like the fellow who was at the funeral of his wife, and the undertaker had asked him if he would ride down to the cemetery in the same car with his mother-in-law. He said, "Well, I can do it, but it's just going to spoil the whole day for me."

September 18, 1948

Republicans don't like people to talk about depressions. You remember the old saying: "Don't talk about rope in the house of somebody who has to be hanged."

In most of my campaigns, I find it best not
to mention my opponent by name because, by
doing so, it just gives him a chance to get into
the headlines.

I have a confession to make to you here
tonight. For the last two or three weeks I've had
a queer feeling that I'm being followed, that
someone is following me. I felt it so strongly
that I went into consultation with the White
House physician. And I told him that I kept
having this feeling, that everywhere I go
there's somebody following behind me. The
White House physician told me not to worry.
He said: "You keep right on your way. There
is one place where that fellow is not going to
follow you—and that's in the White House."

❧

The other day, a cartoonist for a Republican newspaper drew a cartoon of me that I enjoyed. He showed me dressed up as Paul Revere, riding through a colonial town, yelling to the townspeople: "Look out! The Republicans are coming!"

It was a good cartoon. There's a lot of truth in it. But it's not quite accurate. What I am really telling you is not that the Republicans are coming, but that they are here. They have been in Washington for the last two years in the form of the notorious Republican 'do-nothing' Eightieth Congress.

September 20, 1948

Let's take a look at the record of the Eightieth Congress they're so proud of. I call it the "notorious, do-nothing Republican Eightieth Congress." Maybe I ought to leave out the "do-nothing" part of it, because it did do some things—most of them bad.

October 6, 1948

We can take heart from a comment made by that great American heavyweight champion Joe Louis. In one fight, some time ago, he had a hard time catching up with his opponent. But Joe finally did catch up with him, and he knocked him out. After the fight, this is what Joe said: "Well, he could run away, but he couldn't hide."

October 6, 1948

The Republican leadership wouldn't give the American people the kind of housing they need because the rich real estate lobby opposed it. The Hoover slogan, if you remember, back in 1929 and 1930 was, "Two cars in every garage." The Republican slogan today is, "Two families in every garage."

October 7, 1948

The Republican party either corrupts its liberals or it expels them.

GOP these days means just one thing: 'Grand Old Platitudes.'

While Truman was campaigning in Barstow, California, a woman called to him, "President Truman, you sound as if you had a cold."

"That's because I ride around in the wind with my mouth open," the President replied.

In a campaign speech in Idaho Falls, Idaho, Truman joked:

"During the war I was up in Presque Isle, Maine, making an investigation of an airfield, and I heard there was an Idaho boy in the guardhouse. I inquired as to why he was in the guardhouse. He had been on kitchen police and had refused to peel Maine potatoes."

If I keep you standing here in this rain any longer you will be against anything I want, and I wouldn't blame you. But I understand that you need the rain worse than you need to listen to any Presidential speech.

Auburn, New York
October 8, 1948

Now the Republicans tell me that they stand for unity. In the old days, Al Smith would have said, "That's baloney!" Today the Happy Warrior would say, "That's a lot of hooey." And if that rhymes with anything, it's not my fault.

But it is important for the people of this country to recognize that time has not changed the fundamental outlook of the Republican Party. The leopard has not changed his spots; he has merely hired some public relations experts. They have taught him to wear sheep's clothing, and to purr sweet nothings about unity in a soothing voice. But it's the same old leopard.

October 8, 1948

A vote is the best way of getting the kind of country and the kind of world you want.

October 10, 1948

There must be life and hope in government. We must achieve and pioneer in the great frontier of human rights and social justice.

October 13, 1948

True liberalism is more than a matter of words. It demands more than sound effects.

October 13, 1948

I have studied the Republican Party for
years at close hand, in the capital of the United
States. And I have discovered where the Republicans
stand on most of the major issues. Since
they won't tell you themselves, I am going to
tell you:

They approve of the American farmer—but
they are willing to help him go broke.

They stand four-square for the American
home—but not for housing.

They are strong for labor—but they are
stronger for restricting labor's rights.

They favor a minimum wage—the smaller
the minimum the better.

They endorse educational opportunity for
all—but they won't spend money for teachers
or for schools.

They think modern medical care and hospitals
are fine—for people who can afford them.

They approve of social security benefits—so
much so that they took them away from almost
a million people.

They believe in international trade—so much
so that they crippled our reciprocal trade program,
and killed our International Wheat
Agreement.

They favor the admission of displaced persons—but
only within shameful racial and
religious limitations.

They consider electric power a great blessing—but
only when the private power companies
get their rake-off.

They say TVA is wonderful—but we ought never to try it again.

They condemn "cruelly high prices"—but fight to the death every effort to bring them down.

They think the American standard of living is a fine thing—so long as it doesn't spread to all the people.

And they admire the Government of the United States so much that they would like to buy it.

October 13, 1948

Hitler learned that efficiency without justice is a vain thing. Democracy does not work that way. Democracy is a matter of faith—a faith in the soul of man—a faith in human rights. That is the kind of faith that moves mountains—that's the kind of faith that hurled the Iron Range at the Axis and shook the world at Hiroshima. Faith is much more than efficiency. Faith gives value to all things. Without faith, the people perish.

October 13, 1948

A free society requires the supremacy of the civil rather than the military authority.

October 14, 1948

Knowledge is not only the key to power. It is the citadel of human freedom.

October 15, 1948

It isn't important who is ahead at one time or another in either an election or a horse race. It's the horse that comes in first at the finish that counts.

October 17, 1948

A President may dismiss the abuse of scoundrels, but to be denounced by honest men honestly outraged is a test of greatness that none but the strongest men can survive.

October 19, 1948

It is not the hand that signs the laws that holds the destiny of America. It is the hand that casts the ballot.

October 19, 1948

It takes courage to face a duelist with a
pistol and it takes courage to face a British
general with an army. But it takes still greater
and far higher courage to face friends with a
grievance. The bravest thing Andrew Jackson
ever did was to stand up and tell his own people
to their faces that they were wrong.

October 19, 1948

Intense feeling too often obscures the truth.

October 19, 1948

The strength of this Republic lies in the fact
that so many millions of men and women, who
hold no office and aspire to none, recognize as
clearly as Presidents Jackson, Polk, and Johnson did that they must serve their country
before they serve themselves.

October 19, 1948

Polls are like sleeping pills designed to lull the voters into sleeping on Election Day. You might call them 'sleeping polls.'

October 26, 1948

The same doctor I told you about the other night in Pittsburgh—the Republican candidate —keeps handing out these sleeping polls, and some people have been taking them. This doctor keeps telling the people: "Don't worry. Take a poll and go to sleep."

But most of the people are not being fooled. They know that sleeping polls are bad for the system. They affect the mind. An over-dose could be fatal.

My opponent is conducting a very peculiar campaign. He has set himself up as a kind of doctor with a magic cure for all the ills of mankind.

Let's imagine that we, the American people, are going to see this doctor. It's just our usual routine check-up which we have every four years.

We go into the doctor's office.

'Doctor,' we say, 'we're feeling fine.'

'Is that so?' says the doctor. You been bothered much by issues lately?'

'Not bothered, exactly,' we say. 'Of course, we've had quite a few. We've had the issues of high prices, and housing, education and social security, and a few others.'

'That's bad,' says the doctor. 'You shouldn't have so many issues,'

'Is that right?' we say. 'We thought that issues were a sign of political health.'

'Not at all,' says the doctor. 'You shouldn't think about issues. What you need is my brand of soothing syrup—I call it "unity."'

Then the doctor edges up a little closer.

'Say, you don't look so good,' he says.

We say to him, 'Well, that seems strange to me, Doc. I never felt stronger, never had more money, and never had a brighter future. What is wrong with me?'

Well, the doctor looks blank, and says, 'I never discuss issues with a patient. But what you need is a major operation.'

'Will it be serious, Doc?' we say.

'No, not very serious,' he says. 'It will just mean taking out the complete works and putting in a Republican Administration.'

That's the kind of campaign you're getting from the Republicans. They won't talk about the issues, but they insist that a major operation is necesssary.

⚬~⚬

In 1928 the Republicans elected a well-known efficiency engineer named Herbert Hoover, and they promised us everything . . . You know what a bitter experience you had after that. Many of you remember 1932. Over in Central Park men and women were living in little groups of shacks made of cardboard and old boxes. They were known as "Hoovervilles." Out here on Eighth Avenue veterans were selling apples. Ragged individualism, I suppose that's what you would call it.

1948

It only takes one nation to make war. But it
takes two or more to make a peace.

October 27, 1948

I never sit on a fence. I am either on one
side or another.

October 30, 1948

✧✦✧

REPORTER: "Mr. President, you have been reported in a forgiving mood."

PRESIDENT TRUMAN: "That's right."

REPORTER: (Mrs. May Craig of Portland, Maine, *Press-Herald*): "Mr. President, I am anxious to know if there is anybody you are not forgiving?"

PRESIDENT TRUMAN: "I don't know that there is anybody I have anything to forgive, except Maine for not going Democratic."

Press Conference
December 2, 1948

✧✦✧

I travelled up and down the country [in 1948]. . . . I kept my eyes open, as well as an ear to the ground, although I remembered what Hanna said about McKinley. He said that he had his ears so close to the ground that he had them full of grasshoppers. But my hearing didn't get impaired.

∽∾

President Truman's election in 1948 was a surprise victory. To George Allen's candid remark that "I was supremely confident of your defeat," Mr. Truman replied, "So was everybody else. But you're the first one who's admitted it."

∽∾

There is always a letdown after every war, and the Eightieth Congress was the luckiest thing that ever happened to me.

∽∾

At six o'clock I was defeated. At ten o'clock I was defeated. Twelve o'clock, I was defeated. Four o'clock I had won the election. And the next morning . . . in St. Louis, I was handed this paper which said, "DEWEY DEFEATS TRUMAN!" Of course, he wished he had, but he didn't and that's all there was to it.

THE PRESIDENT
AND THE PRESS

REPORTER: "Mr. President, have you read Walter Lippmann's articles on Germany?"

PRESIDENT TRUMAN: "Yes, I have read them."

REPORTER: "Would you care to comment on them?"

PRESIDENT TRUMAN: "Well, as I commented at the Gridiron dinner: hindsight is a great thing."

May 9, 1946

∽∾∿

REPORTER: "Mr. President, do you have any plans to seize the Pittsburgh ball club?"

PRESIDENT TRUMAN: "The Pittsburgh ball club goes on strike?"

REPORTER: "They are going to go out tomorrow night."

PRESIDENT TRUMAN: "Well, I want to say to you that if those ball fellows go on strike, and I have to take them over, I'll have two damn good teams in St. Louis."

June 6, 1946

REPORTER: "Mr. President, you said you hadn't made any advance calculations or bets on the elections. Are you willing to lay a small wager?"

PRESIDENT TRUMAN: "It's contrary to the law in the state of Missouri to make a bet on the election. I expect to vote in the state of Missouri."

REPORTER: "Mr. President, this morning's [Washington] *Post* has an editorial saying it thinks you ought to appoint a lot of Republicans . . ."

PRESIDENT TRUMAN: "I'm a Democrat."

REPORTER: "Mr. President, *The New York Times* this morning has a story out of Paris saying that there is—may be—a drastic change in our foreign policy . . ."

PRESIDENT TRUMAN: "I haven't heard about it, and I make the policy."

REPORTER: "Mr. President, the Republican national campaign director today accuses you of ingannation in connection with your budget."

PRESIDENT TRUMAN: "Well, I guess that's just to add to the obfuscation of all the rest of his statement. That's about in line with what he's trying to say."

REPORTER: "Mr. President, getting back to the ingannation—"

PRESIDENT TRUMAN: "The obfuscation."

REPORTER: "Get him to spell that, will you?"

PRESIDENT TRUMAN: "Well, I will spell it for you. I had it looked up in the dictionary. It means deceit or deception, and it is spelled i-n-g-a-n-n-a-t-i-o-n. I don't use $40 words like that in my language."

REPORTER: "Is that a double n, Mr. President?"

PRESIDENT TRUMAN: "That's a Republican word. It isn't Democratic."

August 9, 1946

REPORTER: "Mr. President, on page 61 of the [Budget] Message, what in heaven's name is antibiotic?"

PRESIDENT TRUMAN: "Well, you will have to ask some expert. [To Mr. Webb, Budget Director] Tell him what it is; I don't know."

DIRECTOR WEBB: "Germ control."

REPORTER: "Well, why not say so?"

PRESIDENT TRUMAN: "We wouldn't have had that good question if that item hadn't been in there."

January 8, 1947

PRESIDENT TRUMAN (being reminded of his reference to cats): "Oh yes. That was at an off-the-record meeting where I read the requests that—if you remember—for all the weeks. Well, one of the requests was for a national cat week, and I thought it was funny!"

REPORTER: "You are not against cats?"

PRESIDENT TRUMAN: "No. Neutral. I am neutral on cats. Certain sort of cats that I am against, but they have two legs."

February 1, 1947

REPORTER: "You are quoted as having said at the last Congressional reception that there are only four [Republicans] you didn't like."

PRESIDENT TRUMAN: "Well, I don't remember that comment. I don't remember that comment."

REPORTER: "Would it be only four, Mr. President?"

PRESIDENT TRUMAN: "Well, I wouldn't like to limit it to four."

February 28, 1947

REPORTER: "Mr. President, have you given any thought to grocery prices?"

PRESIDENT TRUMAN: "I have given it no thought. Only when I go to pay my bill."

April 5, 1947

REPORTER: "Mr. President, you have been in office about a little over two years, and you are having another birthday. Has your philosophy of life changed any in those two years?"

PRESIDENT TRUMAN: "Not the slightest. Not the slightest. I think we have the greatest government in the world. I think we have the greatest government the world has ever seen. The more I become familiar with it, the better I like it, even if it does make a slave out of the President."

May 8, 1947

REPORTER: "Mr. President, there has been some printed speculation that Dr. Steelman might leave your personal staff and head the new Federal Conciliation Service. Would you care to comment on that?"

PRESIDENT TRUMAN: "I hadn't heard about it, and I don't think Dr. Steelman has either. I think he is pretty well satisfied working twenty-four hours a day for me."

July 10, 1947

REPORTER: "Mr. President, have you seen any flying saucers?"

PRESIDENT TRUMAN: "Only in the newspapers."

July 10, 1947

REPORTER: "Mr. President, did Dr. Weizmann suggest a loan to Israel?"

PRESIDENT TRUMAN: "He did not suggest a loan. He said he would like to have a loan, just like every other country. If you know of any countries that wouldn't like to have a loan, I wish you would name them."

May 27, 1948

REPORTER: "Mr. President, have you made any plans to go to New York and New England yet in the campaign?"

PRESIDENT TRUMAN: "I will go to New York on the 31st of July to review the Air Corps. That is not a political trip, however. Mr. Dewey will be there, too."

July 22, 1948

⚬⚬⚬

REPORTER: "Mr. President, Governor Dewey said yesterday that cleaning the Communists out of Washington was a national job of great urgency, and one that should be tackled as soon as a Republican President could get it done. Any comment on that?"

PRESIDENT TRUMAN: "I think Mr. Dewey's intention is to eliminate the Democrats from Government, not the Communists."

September 2, 1948

⚬⚬⚬

REPORTER: "Mr. President, to go back to lobbyists, would you be against lobbyists who are working for your program?"

PRESIDENT TRUMAN: "Well, that's a different matter. We probably wouldn't call these people lobbyists. We would call them citizens appearing in the public interest."

December 2, 1948

REPORTER: "He [Bradley Dewey in *Atlantic Monthly* article] winds up the article by saying that the White House has kept [a report] from the American people for a year."

PRESIDENT TRUMAN: "Mr. Dewey is just mistaken, that's all. That seems to run with the name."

December 2, 1948

REPORTER: "Mr. President, have you read any columns in which you found any truth at all?"

PRESIDENT TRUMAN: "Not lately!"

December 2, 1948

REPORTER: "Mr. President, Mr. Dewey [the 1948 Republican Presidential candidate] was lamenting the fact that the Republican party is split wide open. Do you have any advice for him that would—"

PRESIDENT TRUMAN: "I gave him all the advice I possibly could during the campaign."

February 10, 1949

⟨∾⟩

REPORTER: "Mr. President, I see that among the candidates for the Nobel Peace Prize are President Perón of Argentina and my colleague Mr. Drew Pearson. Were either of them nominated by the government of the United States?"

PRESIDENT TRUMAN: "I can say categorically that they were not. Probably nominated themselves."

February 24, 1949

⟨∾⟩

REPORTER: "Could you say what you and Mr. [Paul E.] Fitzpatrick talked about?"

PRESIDENT TRUMAN: "We talked about politics in the great state of New York. That's what the State Chairman usually talks about with the President of the United States, and he usually is always very anxious to know if there are any good jobs loose."

April 14, 1949

REPORTER: "Mr. President, the first thing Jefferson did [regarding the Alien and Sedition laws] was to release eleven newspaper publishers from prison."

PRESIDENT TRUMAN: "Yes. I think he made a mistake on that."

June 16, 1949

At the end of a press conference when long-awaited news of the President's Supreme Court appointment had finally been given:

REPORTER: "Thank you, Mr. President."

PRESIDENT TRUMAN: "You're welcome. Don't break your legs now."

July 28, 1949

⟜∾⟜

REPORTER: "Mr. President, do you see any improvement in business conditions?"

PRESIDENT TRUMAN: "All I know is what I read in the papers, and even *The Wall Street Journal* says there is an improvement."

August 4, 1949

⟜∾⟜

REPORTER: (referring to a statement that a certain action had been designed to embarrass the President): "I wonder if you felt embarrassed?"

PRESIDENT TRUMAN: "You know I am embarrass-proof."

October 27, 1949

⟜∾⟜

President's opening statement at November 10, 1949, press conference:

"Some of the boys up here in the front row are making fun of my certificate as an honorary airline transport pilot, with all ratings authorized. I was trying this morning to get volunteers for my first flight, and I couldn't get any."

REPORTER: "Mr. President, *The Wall Street Journal* yesterday had a story that the Administration had abandoned its hope of budget balancing, and that there will be no new taxes proposed for next year."

PRESIDENT TRUMAN: "Well now, *The Wall Street Journal* must have been standing behind the curtain somewhere that I know nothing about. No such arrangement has been arrived at."

REPORTER: "They didn't hear it accurately?"

PRESIDENT TRUMAN: "No, sir, they did not hear accurately. They hardly ever do."

November 17, 1949

GENERAL MacARTHUR

Time after time, MacArthur went his own way in national policies. And he didn't seem to care whether he upset the national policy of the Government of the United States or not ... He was trying to get himself in good with one of the big parties of the Government . . . so that he could be President of the United States. He didn't fool anybody—and least of all didn't fool me!

There was a statement that MacArthur stirred things up so that he would be the leader of the disgruntled people who were against what was being done there. Well, I was satisfied that was the case. And it was the last thing in the world that a commanding general of a republic has any right to do.

∽∾

If there is one basic element in our Constitution, it is civilian control of the military. Policies are to be made by elected political officials, not by generals or admirals. Yet time and again General MacArthur had shown that he was unwilling to accept the policies of this administration. By his repeated public statements, he was not only confusing the allies . . . but, in fact, was also setting his policy against the President's.

March, 1951

∽∾

Courage didn't have anything to do with it. General MacArthur was insubordinate and I fired him. That's all there was to it.

∽∾

MacArthur refused to respect the authority of the President. He challenged the traditional civilian supremacy in our government.

He was a very ambitious man. In 1948 he
allowed some Texas millionaires to back him as
a candidate at the Republican convention. A lot
of people wanted to be President in 1948.

When we met on Wake Island, among other
things, he said he wasn't in politics and he had
let the politicians make a 'chump' of him in
1948.

✥

In the first place, of course, he was wrong. I always felt the Soviets were the real aggressors, and they'd be the only winners if we got bogged down in what Bradley called "the wrong war, at the wrong place, at the wrong time, and with the wrong enemy." If MacArthur's advice had been taken we would have been openly at war with Red China, then probably with Russia, and World War III would have been on.

✥

The next morning I got to my office after my walk at about eight-fifteen and George Marshall was already there in the outer office, waiting for me. That was very unusual, because George was a fella who was usually late for meetings. He got to his feet, and he said to me, "I spent most of the night on that file. Mr. President, you should have fired the son-of-a-bitch two years ago!"

～◇～

There were two basic problems. The first had
to do with Chiang Kai-shek and his army, which
I always opposed using and MacArthur wanted
to employ, and later it had to do with how
the fighting was to be conducted in Korea. The
President's purpose was to repel the aggression and preserve the Republic of Korea,
whereas MacArthur's policies would have
brought on World War III.

～◇～

When I got off my plane there he was with
that damned beat-up cap, he didn't have a tie,
and his shirt was unbuttoned. It was arranged
we'd meet later at a Quonset hut, and when I
got there exactly on time, MacArthur hadn't arrived. He kept the President waiting almost
forty minutes. I told him—That may be all
right to do to Harry Truman, but no one shows
such disrespect for his Commander-In-Chief.

ON BEING PRESIDENT

Early in his Presidency, Harry Truman noted that being Chief Executive was like riding a tiger.

"A man has to keep riding or be swallowed."

⚬⚬⚬

If you don't have a good sense of humor, you're in a hell of a fix when you are President of the United States.

October 5, 1947

⚬⚬⚬

The President is virtually in jail. He goes from his study to his office and from his office to his study, and he has to have guards there all the time. And they do a good job, too—I am not criticizing the guards—but when you get out and see people and find out what people are thinking about, you can do a better job as President of the United States.

June 4, 1948

⌒∾⌒

You have to be very careful always to keep
that sense of humor in mind when you are
President of the United States, because if you
don't keep that in mind, you will get a bad case
of "Potomac fever," and then you are ruined.
You know Woodrow Wilson said that a great
many men came to Washington and grew up
with their jobs, and a very large number came
and just swelled up.

June 11, 1948

⌒∾⌒

It's almost impossible for a man to be President of the United States without learning
something.

August 14, 1948

The President spends most of his time kissing people first on one cheek and then on the other in order to get them to do what they ought to do without getting kissed.

February 1, 1949

Addressing the Senate Foreign Relations Committee, April 1955:
"Any man who has had the job I've had and didn't have a sense of humor wouldn't still be here."

There is one thing about this job. It has no future to it. Every young man wants something to look forward to.

❧

The Presidency is a killing job—a six man job. I know, I've been through it. It requires young men—young in physical and mental ability, if not necessarily young in age.

July 1, 1956

❧

Some of the Presidents were great and some of them weren't. I can say that, because I wasn't one of the great Presidents, but I had a good time trying to be one.

April 27, 1959

❧

Some Senators and Congressmen come in and pass the time of day, and then go out and help me save the world in the press.

I am the thirty-second man to be President. If you count the Administration of Grover Cleveland twice because another President held office between Cleveland's first and second terms, you might try to justify the designation of me as thirty-third President. But why don't you number all the second terms of other Presidents and the third and fourth terms of President Roosevelt, and where will you be? I am the thirty-second President.

I hope to go back to the farm some day. Some people are in a hurry for me to go back, but I'm not going back as fast as they want me to.

Truman was once asked to explain his "give 'em hell" speeches. "I never give them hell," said Truman. "I just tell the truth and they think it is hell."

※

At a meeting with General MacArthur, the General took out his pipe, and then asked the President if he minded the smoke.

"No," replied the President, "I suppose I have had more smoke blown at me than any other man alive."

※

After listening to a speech in which James Byrnes lashed out at waste and extravagance in the "welfare state," Truman wrote him a letter in which he said, "Since your speech, I know how Caesar felt when he said, '*Et tu, Brute.*'"

※

We would help to cure senility and seniority —both terrible legislative diseases nationally— if twelve years were the limit of service for President, Senator, and Congressman.

⟨∿⟩

The principal power the President has is to bring people in and try to persuade them to do what they ought to do without persuasion. That's what I spent most of my time doing. That's what the powers of the Presidency amount to.

March 21, 1965

⟨∿⟩

President Truman enjoyed talking about his attempt to join the army during World War II:

"General George Marshall pulled down his specs on the end of his nose, like that, and said, 'How old are you?' I said, 'Well, I am fifty-six.'

" 'Well,' he said, 'you are just too old for this one. This is a young man's war. You had better go back and do your duty in the Senate.'

"And I went back and did the best I could in the Senate, and you see where I got myself by doing it."

⟨∿⟩

If I hadn't been President of the United States, I probably would have ended up a piano player in a bawdy house.

1600 PENNSYLVANIA
AVENUE

Harry Truman commenting on living in the White House:
"The finest prison in the world."

In a letter to his mother, Truman spoke about all the clocks in the White House.
"The ship's clock in Mrs. Wallace's [his mother-in-law] room bangs away in that crazy sailor count of bells. The old grandfather clock in the hall has a high squeaky voice like fat tenors and there is a hoarse clock, a little time-keeper with a big voice—like most small people."

⤙⤛⤜⤙

When President Truman decided to put a new balcony on the White House, it caused immediate controversy, as these excerpts from a press conference on January 15, 1948, indicate:

REPORTER: "Mr. President, are you going ahead with the controversial balcony?"

PRESIDENT TRUMAN: "I am! Your paper to the contrary notwithstanding."

REPORTER: "Mr. President, you indicated that newspapers didn't want to give information about that balcony—do you care to say anything about it?"

PRESIDENT TRUMAN: "I can tell you some other thing. There was the same opposition to putting bathtubs in the White House, and a cooking stove, and gaslight. Mrs. Fillmore put the first bathtub in the White House, but they almost lynched her for doing it."

In a note written on November 1, 1949, Truman humorously comments on the formality of dining at the White House.

"Had dinner by myself tonight. Worked in Lee House office until dinnertime. A butler came in very formally and said, 'Mr. President, dinner is served.' I walked into the dining room in the Blair House. Barnett in tails and white tie pulls out my chair, pushes me up to the table. John in tails and white tie brings me a fruit cup, Barnett takes away the empty cup. John brings me a plate, Barnett brings me a tenderloin. John brings me asparagus, Barnett brings me carrots and beets. I have to eat alone and in silence in candlelit room. I ring. Barnett takes the plate and butter plates. John comes in with a napkin and silver crumb tray—there are no crumbs but John has to brush them off the table anyway. Barnett brings me a plate with a finger bowl and doily on it. I remove the finger bowl and doily and John puts a glass saucer and a little bowl on the plate. Barnett brings me some chocolate custard. John brings me a demitasse (at home a little cup of coffee—about two good gulps) and my dinner is over. I take a hand bath in the finger bowl and go back to work. What a life!"

When Mr. Truman had to move his family out of the White House because of cracking floor beams he remarked:

"My heart trembles when I think of the disasters we might have had with sixteen hundred people at those White House receptions, none of them knowing that the hundred-and-eighty-ton roof might fall on their heads at any moment.

"The only thing that kept the White House up was habit."

Remarking about Margaret Truman's hobby of taking photographs in the White House, Mr. Truman commented:

"It's not enough that my homely countenance is at the mercy of the press—I have to have a photographer in the family."

DIPLOMACY AND DEFENSE

In an address to an American Legion Post in Washington, March, 1938, Senator Truman said:

"I believe in an adequate national defense program. I think that the old Puritan who prayed regularly for protection against the Indians was much safer when, at the same time, he prudently kept his powder dry."

～～～

Just before he left for the Potsdam Conference, Truman wrote to his mother:

"I am getting ready to see Stalin and Churchill and it is a chore. I have to take my tuxedo, tails, preacher coat, high hat, low hat and hard hat."

～～～

On Stalin: "I like Old Joe—not a bad guy when you get a chance to talk face to face."

1945

I like Old Joe. He is a decent fellow. But Joe is a prisoner of the Politburo. He can't do what he wants to. He makes agreements, and if he could he would keep them; but the people who run the government are very specific in saying that he can't keep them.

1945

Mr. Truman enjoyed telling the story about when Stalin gave a dinner at the Potsdam Conference:

"All the Russians were drinking a lot of vodka. Stalin kept pouring all night from a special bottle he had in front of him and drinking one drink after another. Finally I asked if I could taste what he had in that bottle. You know, it was nothing but a light French white wine?"

Relaxing with friends, President Truman was asked to play Paderewski's Minuet.

"When Stalin heard me play this [at Potsdam] he signed the protocol."

No nation on this globe should be more internationally minded than America because it was built by all nations.

March 17, 1945

All Fascism did not die with Mussolini. Hitler is finished—but the seeds spread by his disordered mind have firm root in too many fanatical brains. It is easier to remove tyrants and destroy concentration camps than it is to kill the ideas which gave them birth and strength. Victory on the battlefield was essential, but it was not enough. For a good peace, a lasting peace, the decent peoples of the earth must remain determined to strike down the evil spirit which has hung over the world for the last decade.

June 26, 1945

❦

REPORTER: "Mr. President, do you support the State Department's policy that the United States should—"

PRESIDENT TRUMAN: "The State Department doesn't have a policy unless I support it."

January 31, 1946

❦

In a speech, President Truman quoted Mark Twain: "If we had less statesmanship, we could get along with fewer battleships."

❦

Commenting on military men, Truman said: "There was a remarkable southern general who started as a private at forty-one years of age and ended up as a lieutenant-general when the war was over. He was Nathan Bedford Forrest and he could hardly read or write. One of his lieutenants asked for a leave, and he wrote an endorsement on the request for leave: 'i tole you twicit goddamit no.'"

If Chiang Kai-shek had been willing to listen to General Marshall, General Wedemeyer and General Dean he never would have found himself in the condition he is in now. After the surrender of Peping where ammunition, trucks, and artillery material we have furnished was turned over to the Communists I cut off everything to the Chinese Government. It had to be done gradually, however, because Nationalists were still holding the line of the Yangtze River and I didn't want to pull the rug from under Chiang Kai-shek at that time.

Soviet Foreign Minister Vyacheslov M. Molotov once said to Truman, "I have never been talked to like that in my life." To which Truman told the Foreign Minister: "Carry out your agreement and you won't get talked to like that again."

International relations have traditionally been compared to a chess game in which each nation tries to outwit and checkmate the other.

March 3, 1947

Commenting on a successful visit to Brazil in 1947, President Truman quipped:

"We have never had such a reception. I am tempted to come and run for Mayor of Rio de Janeiro—and I think I could be elected."

Pressure was exerted on President Truman by Jewish leaders for favorable votes for Israel in the United Nations, causing Truman to remark:

"I surely wish God Almighty would give the children of Israel an Isaiah, the Christians a St. Paul, and the sons of Ishmael a peep at the Golden Rule."

❦

Truman's military aide Major General Harry
Vaughn was criticized by columnist Drew Pearson for accepting a medal from Argentine dic-
tator Juan Perón. Truman replied, "I am just as
fond of and just as loyal to my military aide as
I am to the high brass, and want you to dis-
tinctly understand that any s.o.b. who thinks
he can cause any one of these people to be discharged by me by some smart-aleck statement
over the air or in the paper, has got another
think coming."

❦

It is not the martinets that make an army
work; it's the morale that the leaders put into
the men that makes an army work.

October 24, 1950

The United Nations is a mirror in which the state of world affairs is reflected.

May 22, 1950

We can well afford to pay the price of peace. Our only alternate is to pay the terrible cost of war.

August 5, 1951

Speaking of summit conferences . . . I don't believe in them. They don't amount to a damn. I have been to two of them, and nothing was accomplished.

November 4, 1962

PARTY POLITICS

Speaking at a luncheon of the Kansas City Jesters just after he became President, Truman said, "When I hear Republicans say I'm doing all right, I know damned well I'm wrong."

1945

⌇⌇⌇

Political parties are the instruments through which democracy works. Our party system remains as one of the massive foundations of our liberty. Only the free play of political opposition can guarantee the survival of civil freedom.

March 23, 1946

Not long ago, an elderly man who was driving into Gary gave a lift to a young man going his way.

During their talk, the older man asked the young fellow, 'What takes you to Gary?'

The young man hesitated, put his head down, and said: 'I am working for the Republican State Committee. They are sending me to Gary to see what I can do to get the people to vote the Republican ticket.'

The old man was silent for a while, and then he said: 'Son, I've listened to sad stories for fifty years, and that's the saddest one I've heard yet.'

I agree. I can think of no harder job than to try to sell the Republican Party to the men and women of Gary who lived through those dark years of the Republican depression in 1930, 1931, and 1932.

Excerpts from a speech by Mr. Truman at a Jefferson-Jackson Day Dinner, Washington, D.C. on February 24, 1949:

"Once upon a time, there were a number of citizens who thought that Andrew Jackson ought to have a suitable coffin. At great expense, they went to Syria and purchased a marble sarcophagus. A sarcophagus, as you know, is a tomb—a big marble coffin with a marble lid. These citizens then shipped this box to Washington, which was quite a job, as it weighed four or five tons.

"At last, they thought, a suitable resting place had been provided for Andrew Jackson.

"Well, the only trouble with the project was that Andrew Jackson wasn't dead. Moreover, he wasn't ready to die. And he did not intend to be hurried to his grave.

"Courteously but firmly, he wrote to these well-meaning citizens and said, 'I must decline the intended honor.'

"And they never did get Old Hickory into that thing. You can still see it, if you're interested, out in front of the Smithsonian Institution. It still sits there. Andy wouldn't even be buried in it.

"I think that this little story has a moral in it. It is this: Before you offer to bury a good Democrat, you'd better be sure he is dead."

The Republican platform is for extending and increasing social security benefits. Think of that! Increasing social security benefits! Yet when they had the opportunity, they took 750,000 off the social security rolls!

I wonder if they think they can fool the people of the United States with such poppycock as that!

There is a long list of these promises in that Republican platform. If it weren't so late, I would tell you all about them. I have discussed a number of these failures of the Republican Eightieth Congress. Every one of them is important. Two of them are of major concern to nearly every American family. They failed to do anything about high prices, they failed to do anything about housing.

My duty as President requires that I use every means within my power to get the laws the people need on matters of such importance and urgency.

I am therefore calling this Congress back into session July 26th.

On the 26th day of July, which out in Missouri we call 'Turnip Day,' I am going to call Congress back and ask them to pass laws to halt rising prices, to meet the housing crisis—which they are saying they are for in their platform.

At the same time I shall ask them to act upon
other vitally needed measures such as aid to
education, which they say they are for; a
national health program; civil rights legis-
lation, which they say they are for; and an
increase in the minimum wage, which I doubt
very much they are for.

I have often wondered what a so-called lib-
eral Republican thinks. On election year they
call him out and pat him on the back, and send
him around over the country to make speeches
in support of a platform that he doesn't believe
in—and just as soon as the election is over, they
put him back in the doghouse, and he votes with
the Democrats for the rest of the time.

May 14, 1948

❧❧❧

What did the Republicans do with my proposal for health insurance? You can guess. They did nothing.

All they said was 'Sorry. We can't do that. The medical lobby says it's un-American.'

The Governor of the state of New York now wants to be President. He was asked right at the height of the fight in Congress what he thought about the Taft-Ellender-Wagner Bill. Do you know what he said? He said, 'I haven't had time to read it.' Well, he pretends to know something about housing, but if he's too busy to read the bill that would have made the difference between houses and no houses, then he doesn't know much.

❧❧❧

The Republican platform comes out for slum clearance and low-rental housing. I have been trying to get them to pass that housing bill ever since they met the first time, and it is still resting in the Rules Committee, that bill.

The Republican platform favors educational opportunity and promotion of education. I have been trying to get Congress to do something about that ever since they came there, and that bill is at rest in the House of Representatives.

The less harmony there is in the Republican Party, the better suited I am.

July 14, 1949

Speaking in St. Paul, Minnesota, on the occasion of the hundredth anniversary of Minnesota as a territory, Truman told his audience:
"I have to deliver an address of a bipartisan nature that will be entirely satisfactory to the Democrats of Minnesota."

November 14, 1949

A sound government to the Republican is the kind of government where the President makes nice sounds while the Vice-President snarls.

The Republicans have General Motors and General Electric and General Foods and General MacArthur and General Martin and General Wedemeyer. And they have their own five-star general running for President . . . I want to say to you that every general I know is on this list except general welfare, and general welfare is in with the corporals and privates in the Democratic Party.

1952

Truman commented on Dwight Eisenhower's actions in the campaign of 1952: "Hard as it was for us to understand this side of Eisenhower now revealed to us, it was even more of a jolt to see our foreign policy used as a political football."

Truman was known to refer to Eisenhower as ". . . that fella who succeeded me."

A powerful group of men in the Republican
Party is now determined to rise to power
through a method of conduct as hostile to
American ideals as anything we have seen.
This method has come to be known as
McCarthyism.

It is our duty to win if we can—for the
simple reason that the principles and programs
of the Democratic party are what's best for the
United States.

Addressing Democratic Rally in Chicago
September, 1953

❦

I don't like bipartisans. Whenever a fellow tells me he's bipartisan, I know he's going to vote against me.

❦

When a leader is in the Democratic Party he's a boss. When he's in the Republican Party he's nothing but a leader. But there's no difference in them.

❦

In 1940, the Republicans had a poll that told them they had the edge. Well, it was a mighty sharp edge. They got cut to ribbons on election day.

❧

Don't let the Republicans fool you with their smooth talk about what they are going to do for the farmers and the workers and the small businessmen of this country.

Their actions speak louder than words. You know, Uncle Joe Cannon had quite a career in this great town [Danville], and he was present when one of your colleagues said he would rather be right than President. Old Uncle Joe made a famous answer. He said: "I am sure that my worthy friend will never be right, or President either."

I think that is absolutely true of the Republicans today. They will never be right, and they will never elect a President if the people understand what they are trying to do.

❧

A young boy once asked Truman the difference between Democrats and Republicans.

"Democrats work to help people who need help," he replied. "That other party, they work for people who don't need help. That's all there's to it."

"Then how come so many Republicans are elected to office?" the boy questioned.

"Because they had the most votes!" Mr. Truman responded.

I want to read you something here that is just as interesting as it can be—I don't think I have ever seen anything as interesting. Now, this is called *The Republican News*. It is the official publication of the Republican Party. Now, I want to read you something because it is very enlightening. It is exceedingly enlightening, and it is terrible for the country.

Here it is: "Don't Throw Peanuts to the Elephant!" Wait a minute—you will find out what the "peanuts" means. Take a look: "Many of our friends feel that, entirely apart from other important considerations, the least they can do to express their appreciation is to contribute a substantial part of their tax savings for this year to insure the re-election of the Congress which made this possible."

That is the terrible Eightieth Congress they are talking about, that didn't do anything for the country.

WASHINGTON, D.C.,
AND THE WORLD
FROM INDEPENDENCE, MO.

McCarthyism: the meaning of the word is the corruption of truth, the abandonment of our historical devotion to fair play. It is the abandonment of "due process" of law. It is the use of the big lie and the unfounded accusation against any citizen in the name of Americanism and security. It is the rise to power of the demagogue who lives on untruth; it is the spread of fear and the destruction of faith in every level of our society . . . This horrible cancer is eating at the vitals of America and it can destroy the great edifice of freedom.

November 17, 1953

No conversation is sweeter than that of former political enemies.

April, 1954

I like Ike, but not as President. He has gotten mixed up with those damn Republicans and doesn't know which way is up.

October, 1956

If civilization is to continue, the people of the world must have a moral code by which to live, and on which to act.

December, 1956

If you want an efficient government, why then go someplace where they have a dictatorship and you'll get it.

April 28, 1959

Nelson Rockefeller . . . He's a very fine man. He did several good things for me when I was President. The only thing I have against him is he's a Republican.

November 29, 1959

The real trouble with Adlai Stevenson . . . the real damn trouble is, he's no better than a regular sissy.

On Castro: ". . . I'd've given him a big reception. I'd've had our picture taken together, then said to him, 'Fidel, you're a nice boy, and so far you've done a pretty good job. Now go back to Havana, shave, change those dirty clothes, and leave everything else up to me."

On Bernard M. Baruch: "He had always seen to it that his suggestions and recommendations, not always requested by the President, would be given publicity . . . Baruch is the only man to my knowledge who has built a reputation on a self-assumed unofficial status as 'advisor'."

Speaking of candidates for the Presidency:
"First, he should be an honorable man. Then he
should be a man who can get elected. Finally,
he should be a man who knows what to do after
he is elected."

May 1, 1960

In 1960, Harry Truman was not sure John
F. Kennedy should be President. His worry was
not Kennedy's religion but the possibility of his
father's influence:
"It's not the Pope who worries me, it's the
Pop."

Speaking of Mr. Nixon: "You don't set a
fox to watching the chickens just because he
has a lot of experience in the henhouse."

October 30, 1960

On J.F. Kennedy: "I think that young fella
might just make a hell of a fine President."

Harry Truman commented very infrequently on
Richard M. Nixon. Once, however, he was
quoted by the Associated Press as saying that
anyone who voted for Nixon and Lodge "ought
to go to hell." He added, "and Nixon never told
the truth in his life."

Oct. 10, 1960

I am sure that all of you know that before the Democratic convention made its choice, I was supporting another candidate. At the convention, Jack Kennedy won the nomination. I'm from Missouri, you know, and I have to be shown. Well, Kennedy showed me.

1960

The difficulty with businessmen entering politics, after they have had a successful business career, is that they want to start at the top.

November, 1962

Speaking at a banquet Mr. Truman "corrected" a speaker who had said the judiciary was the most important branch of government.

"The legislative is! It's close to the people and provides the money to run the government. I can say anything I want to about judges, because I have no license to practice law. Therefore, no license can be taken away from me. Besides, I can't be sued, because I haven't anything."

France has been experiencing a terrible inferiority complex and is still trying to get over it.

October 20, 1963

Some of those that could not defend themselves against invasion have grown vain and inflated and are now turning their backs on us. It is not a pretty picture where those whom we have helped to rescue only yesterday are now deliberately trying to do us harm.

February, 1965

⚬⚬⚬

The military men that we have had for Presidents were not successes, I can tell you that. There was General Grant—and the very recent one, about whom I hesitate to talk now—his name was General Eisenhower.

⚬⚬⚬

I don't believe the USA wants any more fakers—Teddy and Franklin are enough.

⚬⚬⚬

World conditions . . . It's bound to be improving or it would have blown up long ago.

July, 1965

⚬⚬⚬

It's a lot tougher to be a football coach than a President. You've got four years as a President, and they guard you. A coach doesn't have anyone to protect him when things go wrong.

September 19, 1965

Memories are short, and appetites for power
and glory are insatiable. Old tyrants depart.
New ones take their places. Old differences are
composed, new differences arise. Old allies
become the foe. The recent enemy becomes the
friend. It is all very baffling and trying . . .
but . . . we cannot lose hope, we cannot de-
spair. For it is all too obvious that if we do not
abolish war on this earth, then surely, one day,
war will abolish us from the earth.

September, 1965

THOUGHTS ON AMERICA

We are strong because of many things: our natural resources which we have so diligently developed; our great farms and mines, our factories, shipyards and industries which we have so energetically created and operated. But above all else, we are strong because of the courage and vigor and skill of a liberty loving people who are determined that this nation shall remain forever free.

October 23, 1945

❧

Our country is not merely the sum of its parts. It is not the total of its resources, the aggregate of its wealth. Our country is much more than the complement of all our states and boundaries, our cities and our farms. It is the sum of its culture, its heritage, its traditions. It is the sum of its strength, its vigor, and its spirit.

January 30, 1946

We have this America not because we are of a particular faith, not because our ancestors sailed from a particular foreign port. We have our America because of our common aspiration to remain free and our determined purpose to achieve for ourselves, and for our children, a more abundant life in keeping with our highest ideals.

March 6, 1946

I think it was my predecessor who said that Americanism is not a matter of race or creed, it is a matter of the heart.

July 15, 1946

We should not forget that our Nation was founded by immigrants, many of whom fled oppression and persecution. We have thrived on the energy and diversity of many peoples. It is a source of our strength that we number among our people all the major religions, races and national origins.

July 7, 1947

America was not built on fear. America was built on courage, on imagination and an unbeatable determination to do the job at hand.

                                    January 8, 1947

America has long been a symbol of freedom and democratic progress to people less favored than we have been. We must maintain their belief in us by our policies and our acts.

                                    February 5, 1947

We are a diverse people, and in this diversity we have great strength. We have room for differences and room for disagreement. Part of our respect for the dignity of the human being is the respect for his right to be different. That means different in background, different in his beliefs, different in his customs, different in his name, and different in his religion. That is true Americanism; that is true democracy. It is the source of our strength. It is the basis of our faith in the future. It is our hope, and it is the hope of the world.

June 4, 1948

We owe to future generations the bequest of a strong America, mighty in its resources and wise in its use of them. We are firmly determined to leave after us a land that is better than we found it.

September 18, 1948

This nation is no wiser than the education of its citizens. This nation is no stronger than the health of its citizens. This nation's security begins with the welfare of its citizens.

October 15, 1948

Americanism is not embodied in any one man. It is a distillation of the spirits of all the heroes who have labored and fought and died for the common good.

October 19, 1948

The American people cannot afford to trust their future to men of little vision. The Bible warns us that where there is no vision the people perish.

October 25, 1948

You know that being an American is more than a matter of where you or your parents came from. It is a belief that all men are created free and equal and that everyone deserves an even break. It is a respect for the the dignity of men and women without regard to race, creed, or color. That is our creed.

October 26, 1948

The little fellow is the backbone of this country.

September 18, 1949

If people couldn't blow off steam they might explode. Half the fun of being a citizen in this country comes from complaining about the way we run our government—state, federal and local.

September 16, 1951

America is dedicated to the conviction that all people are entitled by the gift of God to equal rights and freedoms even though they may differ in religious persuasion, in social and political views, or in racial origin. Our greatness is and will be measured by the degree of our recognition of this fundamental truth.

October 5, 1949

The spirit and the meaning of our courts do not lie in the material settings we provide for them, but in the living ideas which they enshrine.

June 27, 1950

The good society we are seeking is based on order and peaceful cooperation, among men who share common ideals of freedom and justice. All these things are not easy to attain. For a society is made up of men, who are often weak, and selfish, and quarrelsome. And yet, men are the children of God. Men have within them the Divine spark that can lead them to truth, and unselfishness, and courage to do the right. Men can build a good society, if they follow the will of the Lord. Our great Nation was founded on this faith. Our Constitution and all our finest traditions rest on a moral basis.

May 11, 1950

SOME HISTORY LESSONS

At a press conference, Mr. Truman made this comment to May Craig of the Portland, Maine, *Press-Herald:*

"The Chesapeake and Potomac Canal used to run down along there [indicating southern White House grounds] and John Quincy Adams used to go down there and swim every morning. Some lady reporter [Anne Royall] had been trying to get an interview with him for a long time. She went down and sat on his clothes and let him talk to her. I thought you would be interested in that."

McKinley was sometimes described as "the President Mark Hanna made," Hanna being the millionaire Senator from Cleveland who virtually bought the election while McKinley stayed at home and spoke only to such delegations as came to his house from time to time."

1948

❦

John Adams and Thomas Jefferson were political enemies, but they became fast friends.
And when they passed away on the same day,
the last words of one of them was, "The country
is safe. Jefferson still lives." And the last words
of the other was, "John Adams will see that
things go forward."

October 28, 1948

❦

Jesse James was actually not a bad man at
heart. I have studied his life carefully, and I
come from his part of the country. James was a
modernday Robin Hood. He stole from the rich
and gave to the poor, which, in general, is not a
bad policy. I am convinced that James would
have been an asset to his community, if he had
not been diverted into the lawless life.

March 27, 1949

✦~~✦

Franklin Pierce . . . was absolutely a 'do-nothing' President. He'd been a brigadier general in the Mexican War. Whenever there was a big fight on, he took sick . . . Jackson told South Carolina that if they did not enforce the laws in their state, he'd come down and hang every one of them. And they knew he'd do it . . .

✦~~✦

Speaking to the National Cartoonist Association, President Truman debunked the old legend of George Washington's throwing a silver dollar across the Potomac:

"It was a Spanish piece of eight and it was thrown across the Rappahannock. Any ten-year-old boy could throw a dime across at that place. But I am doubtful that Washington with his acquisitive habits, would ever let loose of a Spanish piece of eight."

November 19, 1951

At a White House staff meeting, Truman told
the following story, which he said had been at-
tributed apocryphally to Calvin Coolidge:

"A President was going over detailed matters of state with his staff. Happening to glance
out the window just as the Vice-President
sauntered by the White House, he said, 'There
goes the Vice-President, with nothing on his
mind but the health of the President.'"

Mr. Truman remarked about the relationship
of President and Cabinet. He told how Abraham
Lincoln had once settled a Cabinet argument:
"Well, there's only one decided vote. The vote
is aye."

THE PRIVATE TRUMAN

Mr. Truman once remarked in describing himself, "I look just like any other fifty people you meet in the street."

⟨✦⟩

You know, I went to Sunday school right across there—the first time in my life, a long, long time ago and in that Sunday school class I met a little, blue-eyed, golden-haired girl—my first sweetheart. Her eyes are still blue, but her hair is no longer golden; it's silver—like mine. And she is still my sweetheart.

November 6, 1950

⟨✦⟩

When he interrupted a vacation in Florida to attend a dinner given by the Women's National Democratic Club, President Truman explained:

"Mrs. Truman made this engagement for the two of us; and when I have a date with Mrs. Truman, I usually keep it."

Upon their return to Independence, after
they left the White House, the Trumans were
warmly greeted by their neighbors.

Mr. Truman responded:

"After I get finished with the job Mrs. Truman has for me—unpacking—I'll be open for
dinner engagements. I may be hungry—I don't
have a job."

I am now in the army of unemployed *presidents*. But it is a very small army.

February 1, 1953

Harry Truman commented in 1953 that he
had received more than 70,000 letters since he
left the White House.

"All except about a hundred were favorable,"
Truman commented, "and those few, of course,
were from friends."

I have grown up to look for the good in people. I have never regarded people with suspicion. Such an attitude usually leads to worrying into being a pessimist about everything, people included.

November, 1953

Sometimes I wish I hadn't undertaken my doggone memoirs. By the time I finish paying taxes, I won't have any profit from them.

January 31, 1954

On his seventieth birthday—May 7, 1954—Harry Truman remarked:

"When you become forty, you should take it a little slower, work a little harder, take a little more time to think, and you will be all right. I guess the best assurance of a long life is to get yourself a set of long-living parents like I did."

As you get older, you get tired of doing the same things over and over again, so you think Christmas has changed. It hasn't. It's you who has changed.

December, 1955

I am not an elder statesman. I hate elder statesmen. I am a Democrat and a politician and I'm proud of it.

April 15, 1956

My grandson was on the front page of newspapers when he was only three days old. It took me fifty years to make it.

June 23, 1957

President Truman once told a group of friends of a story he had read in the papers "where a man had called the doctor about three o'clock in the morning and said that his wife had appendicitis and that he wished the doctor would come immediately and do something about it. The doctor told the man to give his wife bicarbonate of soda—that he knew very well that she didn't have two appendixes, as he had taken one out just three years before. The man came back with the statement that he knew a woman couldn't have two appendixes but a man could have two wives in three years."

Responding to a comment that his father, John Anderson Truman, had been a failure in life, Truman remarked:

"My father was not a failure. After all, he was the father of a President of the United States."

❧

Margaret Truman served as the interviewer
on the television program *Person to Person*
on May 27, 1955, substituting for Edward R.
Murrow. Her guests were the President and
Mrs. Truman.

MISS TRUMAN: "Brace yourself."
MR. TRUMAN: "For what?"

❧

MISS TRUMAN: "Everyone who stopped
at the house in Independence in recent years
knows we have a big iron fence around the
property with a gate that opens only when we
push a button in the house. Dad, why don't you
explain why you have that fence out there?"
MR. TRUMAN: "Well, the fence had to be
put up to offset the American propensity for
collecting souvenirs. When I was in the First
World War, it was said that the British fought
for control of the seas, the French for the
freedom of France, and Americans fought for
souvenirs, and they are still fighting for them."

MISS TRUMAN: "I am frequently asked what kind of work—manual work, that is—you do around the house."

MR. TRUMAN: "I do an immense amount of it from a rocking chair."

When asked about his physical exercise, President Truman said that he had never played tennis and was "not old enough yet to take up golf."

Truman was once asked if he could play poker:

"I have played a game where you put the first card face down and the others face up. Then everybody bets, and you turn your hold card up—and somebody takes the money."

I learned to play poker in France—but it was a costly education.

❧❧❧

I don't pretend to be a philosopher. I'm just a politician from Missouri and proud of it.

October 23, 1955

❧❧❧

Fiercely loyal to his state of Missouri, which John Gunther has called "the crossroads of the nation," Mr. Truman, visited by the famous author, pointed to the state on a map and maintained that Missouri was the only state in the Union which could get along even if a fence were built around it.

Turning to Mr. Gunther, he added laughingly, "And Missourians are ornery folks—against everybody."

Mr. Gunther asked pointedly, "What are they for?"

"Missouri," Mr. Truman happily replied.

❧❧❧

Missouri has produced three notorious characters—Mark Twain, Jesse James, and me. Mark and Jesse are dead, but I'm still here filling in for them.

Truman enjoyed telling stories from his youth, such as the following story, which was told to him by his uncle, Harrison Young.

"He told me a story about a pal of his who had the record on a bet by eating thirteen roasting ears of corn. This fellow contracted a stomach ache and he had to send for a doctor. The doctor worked over him the rest of the night and in the morning told him that he had better send for the preacher and do a little praying. The man was in such pain that he sent for the parson. The parson prayed for him and recommended that he also pray for himself.

"But the stricken man told the preacher he was not a praying man and did not think he could do it. However, as the excruciating pain persisted, the man decided to make an attempt. He got down on his knees in the old-fashioned revival manner and this was his petition to the Almighty: 'O Lord I am in great pain and misery. I have eaten thirteen roasting ears of corn and I don't seem to be able to take care of them. I am praying to you for help. And, Lord, I am not like those howling church members in the Amen corner. If you will relieve me of seven of these ears of corn, I will try to handle the other six by myself.' "

The difficulty with the Missouri River is from Sioux City to St. Louis it is a mud river—carries more silt than any other river in the world. Even the Yangtze doesn't carry any more silt than the Missouri. Mark Twain once said that in a wet season you could pour the water of the Missouri from one vessel to the other, if you pushed it and stirred it around enough.

Our young people know a good deal more about everything than the people who are criticizing them.

December 6, 1959

I have found the best way to give advice to your children is to find out what they want and then advise them to do it.

I have had enough experience in all my years, and have read enough of the past, to know that advice to grandchildren is usually wasted. If the second and third generations *could* profit by the experience of the first generation, we would not be having some of the troubles we have today.

1960

I do not like to hunt animals, and I never have. I do not believe in shooting at anything that cannot shoot back.

1960

Truman was the subject of highly laudatory speeches when he visited New York in April, 1965, to receive the annual Freedom House award.

Commenting on all the nice things that had been said about him, Truman quipped:

"You don't know how overcome I am. You don't know how difficult it is to be present at your own funeral and still be able to walk around."

Harry Truman visited New York and was met at the airport by his daughter and her husband Clifton Daniels.

Asked how long he would stay in the city Mr. Truman said: "I'll be here for six days, or until my son-in-law gets tired of me."

August 16, 1965

President Truman was once asked by a friend about the famous photograph of him playing the piano with actress Lauren Bacall sitting on the piano top. "What did Bess [Mrs. Truman] say when she saw the picture?"

"Well," the President answered, "she said maybe it was time for me to quit playing the piano."

∽∾∾

Question: "What kind of music do you like best?"

President Truman: "I am very fond of piano music, particularly. I like Chopin, Mozart, and Beethoven. I am very fond of Gilbert and Sullivan operas, and Verdi operas. Most any kind of music I like except noise. I don't like noise."

∽∾∾

In a letter to music critic Paul Hume, who had written of Margaret Truman's "flat" singing at Constitution Hall a couple of days before, Truman said, "You sound like an eight-ulcer man on a four-ulcer job."

∽∾∾

Maybe the country would have been better off if I had been a concert pianist.

July 1, 1962

A man cannot have character unless he lives within a fundamental system of morals that creates character.

Everybody is headed for the same place, and they are headed on the same train, and under the same engineer.

ONE NATION,
   under God, indivisible,
      with liberty and justice for all

All will concede that in order to have good neighbors, we must also be good neighbors. That applies in every field of human endeavor.

April 25, 1945

∞≈∞

If men and nations would but live by the precepts of the ancient prophets and the teachings of the Sermon on the Mount, problems which now seem so difficult would soon disappear.

March 6, 1946

∞≈∞

I fear we are too much concerned with material things to remember that our real strength lies in spiritual values. I doubt whether there is in this troubled world today, when nations are divided by jealousy and suspicion, a single problem that could not be solved if approached in the spirit of the Sermon on the Mount.

May 11, 1946

I want our Bill of Rights implemented in fact.
We have been trying to do this for 150 years.
We are making progress, but we are not making
progress fast enough. This country could very
easily be faced with a situation similar to the
one with which it was faced in 1922. That date
was impressed on my mind because I was running for my first elective office—county judge
of Jackson County—and there was an organization in that county that met on hills and
burned crosses and worked behind sheets. There
is a tendency in this country for that situation
to develop again, unless we do something tangi-
ble to prevent it.

                                        January 15, 1947

What is good for some people in a community is good for all. What harms some, harms all.

September 26, 1947

Every man should have the right to a decent home, the right to an education, the right to adequate medical care, the right to a worth-while job, the right to an equal share in the making of public decisions through the ballot and the right to a fair trial in a fair court.

July 6, 1947

In our generous impulses we should follow the admonition set forth in St. Matthew's Gospel. Our Lord, bidding us to aid and comfort our stricken neighbor, whoever he may be, spoke words as true today as when He uttered them more than nineteen hundred years ago: "Inasmuch as ye have done it unto one of the least of these my brethren, ye have done it unto me."

September 26, 1947

Differing languages and differing cultural backgrounds are not an obstacle to democratic unity. Such differences can provide the basis for a richer and stronger democracy. "Freedom" is a word which is found in every language. "Equality" means more than mere political emancipation.

February 21, 1948

The farmer, the workingman, and the businessman must prosper together, or they go down together.

June 5, 1948

Racial and religious oppression—big business domination—inflation—these forces must be stopped and driven back while there is yet time.

October 25, 1948

The persecution of minorities goes hand in hand with the destruction of liberty.

October 25, 1948

Only by helping the least fortunate of its members to help themselves, can the human family achieve the decent, satisfying life that is the right of all people.

January 20, 1949

The only sure bedrock of human brotherhood is the knowledge that God is the Father of mankind.

November 11, 1949

Until the captive peoples of the world emerge from darkness, they cannot see the hand we hold out in friendship.

January 1, 1950

The friendless, the weak, the victims of prejudice and public excitement are entitled to the same quality of justice and fair play that the rich, the powerful, the well-connected, and the fellow with pull, thinks he can get.

February 15, 1950

Human life is something that comes to us from beyond this world, and the purpose of our society is to cherish it and to enable the individual to attain the highest achievement of which he is capable . . . Human life is God-given and infinitely valuable.

August 9, 1950

Material things are ashes, if there is no spiritual background for the support of those material things.

June 7, 1950

The basis of mental and moral strength for our children lies in spiritual things. It lies first of all in the home. And next, it lies in the religious and moral influences which are brought to bear on the children. If children have a good home—a home in which they are loved and understood—and if they have good teachers in the first few grades of school, I believe they are well started on the way toward being useful and honorable citizens.

December 5, 1950

I do not think I am being old-fashioned when I say that children ought to have religious training when they are young, and that they will be happier for it and better for it the rest of their lives.

December 5, 1950

The unity of our country is a unity under God. It is a unity in freedom, for the service of God is perfect freedom.

February 3, 1951

In our countries we do not measure our prosperity by the power of the state. We do not measure the progress of our society in terms of military might. We do not measure our advancement in terms of the profits or the luxuries of the few. Our yardstick is the welfare of the many. We think in terms of the average man—how he lives, what he can buy, and the freedom he enjoys. These are the standards by which we measure our development.

March 26, 1951

Freedom is still expensive. It still costs money. It still costs blood. It still calls for courage and endurance, not only in soldiers, but in every man and woman who is free and who is determined to remain free. Freedom must be fought for today, just as our fathers had to fight for freedom when the Nation was born.

July 4, 1951

The worst danger we face is the danger of being paralyzed by doubts and fears. This danger is brought on by those who abandon faith and sneer at hope. It is brought on by those who spread cynicism and distrust and try to blind us to our great chance to do good for all mankind.

October 15, 1951

We must remember that the test of our religious principles lies not just in what we say, not only in our prayers, not even in living blameless personal lives—but in what we do for others.

September 28, 1951

If we are to respond to our religious heritage, we must be guided by the principle of charity— charity in the biblical sense of love for one's fellow man. This is the greatest virtue, without which other virtues are of little worth.

September 28, 1951

THE LIFE AND CAREER OF HARRY S. TRUMAN

May 8, 1884: John Anderson Truman and Mary Ellen Young Truman gave birth to their first son, Harry S. Truman. He was born in Lamar, Missouri.

December 28, 1890: The Truman family moved to Independence, Missouri, where John Truman purchased a small farm. Harry assisted his father with the daily chores on the farm.

September, 1892: Harry Truman entered public school in Independence, Missouri where he was regarded as a bright student by his teachers.

1901: Harry graduated from high school at the age of seventeen.

June 14, 1905: He joined the Missouri National Guard as a member of Battery B.

1906: Truman served as an election clerk where he first came into contact with the Pendergast political machine which controlled Democratic politics in much of Missouri, and later helped him become a U.S. Senator.

June 22, 1917: He was commissioned a first lieutenant in the National Guard.

July 11, 1918: Truman took command of Battery D, 129th Field Artillery as a captain.

September 6, 1918: He experienced his first combat in the Vosges Mountains in the province of Alsace during World War I.

May 6, 1919: He was discharged from the army with the rank of major.

June 28, 1919: At the age of thirty-five, Truman married the former Elizabeth Virginia Wallace (Bess), his childhood sweetheart, in Independence, Missouri.

November 29, 1919: He opened a men's haberdashery in Independence which proved to be a financial failure, leaving Truman with a total of about $20,000 in debts in 1921. Truman, refusing to declare bankruptcy, eventually paid back all of these debts.

November 7, 1922: Truman was elected judge in the County Court (an administrative, not judicial position) in Jackson County, Mo. During this time, he attended the Kansas City School of Law.

February 17, 1924: His only daughter, Mary Margaret, was born.

November 4, 1924: Truman was defeated when he ran for reelection as a county judge. This was to be his only unsuccessful election.

November 2, 1926: He was elected Presiding Judge of Jackson County, Mo.

January 3, 1935: Truman began his first term as a United States Senator from Missouri. In his first term he worked on the Appropriations and Interstate Commerce Committees, as well as serving as Vice Chairman of the Senate subcommittee investigating railroad financing.

November 5, 1940: Truman was reelected to the Senate. As a second term senator, Truman was chairman of the Special Senate Committee to Investigate the National Defense Program (the "Truman Committee"). His committee revealed great waste in government programs.

July 21, 1944: He was nominated for Vice-President at the Democratic National Convention held in Chicago.

November 7, 1944: He was elected Vice-President. Franklin D. Roosevelt was elected President.

April 12, 1945: Franklin D. Roosevelt died, and Harry S. Truman became the thirty-third President of the United States. The oath of office was administered by Chief Justice Harlan Fiske Stone.

April 14, 1945: Truman moved into the Blair House, the President's guest house, while the White House was undergoing extensive renovation.

April 17, 1945: Truman held his first press conference as President.

April 25, 1945: Truman was briefed, for the first time, on the atomic bomb project by Secretary of War Stanton.

April 25, 1945: Truman addressed the U.N. Conference on International Organization in San Francisco, calling for the formation of an organization to insure future peace.

May 8, 1945: Truman announced the cessation of hostilities in Europe and the surrender of Germany in a special radio broadcast to the nation.

June 26, 1945: Truman witnessed the signing of the charter of the United Nations in San Francisco.

July 15, 1945: He arrived in Antwerp, Belgium for the Potsdam conference between the allied nations.

July 16, 1945: He was informed of the successful atomic bomb explosion at Alamogordo, New Mexico.

July 26, 1945: Winston Churchill and Harry Truman issued a joint declaration calling, once more, for the unconditional surrender of Japan.

August 6, 1945: "We have spent $2,000,000,-000 on the greatest scientific gamble in history, and won," Truman announced sixteen hours after the first atomic bomb was dropped on Hiroshima, Japan.

August 8, 1945: Truman signed the United Nations charter.

August 9, 1945: The second atomic bomb was dropped on Nagasaki, Japan.

August 14, 1945: Japan surrendered unconditionally.

September 1, 1945: Truman issued a proclamation in which he urged Americans to observe V-J day as a symbol of "victory of liberty over tyranny."

September 21, 1945: With the acceptance of the resignation of Secretary of War Stimson, Truman approved the recommendation made by Stimson that the war be officially designated World War II.

October 3, 1945: To cope with the new atomic age, Truman sent a special message to Congress urging the formation of the Atomic Energy Commission.

November 10, 1945: Truman appointed General Eisenhower as Chief of the Army.

December 31, 1946: Truman issued an executive proclamation officially ending World War II.

March 12, 1947: Truman sent to Congress his "Truman Doctrine," which was to provide $400,000,000 in economic and military aid to Greece and Turkey so that they would be able to resist "attempted subjugation by armed minorities or by outside pressures."

June 14, 1947: He signed peace treaties with Italy, Hungary, Rumania, and Bulgaria.

May 14, 1948: Truman recognized the newly created State of Israel.

January 1, 1949: He recognized the Republic of Korea.

January 20, 1949: After defeating Thomas Dewey by over two million votes, Truman took the oath of office, administered by Chief Justice Frederick Morre Vinson. He was now 64.

April 4, 1949: He attended the signing of the North Atlantic Treaty in Washington, D.C.

September 23, 1949: Truman announced that the Soviet Union also possessed the atomic bomb.

January 31, 1950: Truman announced that he had told the Atomic Energy Commission to proceed with plans for the production of the H-bomb.

November 1, 1950: An unsuccessful assassination attempt was made on the life of Harry S. Truman by Puerto Rican nationals.

November 26, 1950: Chinese communists entered the Korean war, driving back U.S. forces.

December 16, 1950: Truman declared a national state of emergency.

April 11, 1951: Truman relieved General MacArthur of his Far Eastern command because of failure to follow presidental directives.

March 29, 1952: Truman announced that he would not seek reelection.

June 14, 1952: He dedicated the first nuclear submarine, the Nautilus.

December 26, 1953: In a review of his years as President, Truman stated that his most important decision had been the U.S. intervention into Korea.

December 26, 1972: In Kansas City, Missouri, at the age of eighty-eight, Harry S. Truman died.

Consumer-Protection Guides

THE CONSUMER'S FIGHT-BACK BOOK   James Lewis
This manual, written by an expert on consumer problems, tells you how to protect yourself and fight back—through government agencies, legal means, and just plain consumer-sense.   AN1015—95¢

THE CONSUMER'S HANDBOOK OF BETTER LIVING
Over 1000 ways to save money, time and effort in running you home—by top government specialists!   AQ0585—$1.2*

**CONSUMER SWINDLERS
AND HOW TO AVOID THEM**   John L. Springe*
Learn to protect yourself against repair gyps, investmen* rackets, medical quackery *and more* . . .   AN0737—95*

CAN YOU BE SURE OF YOUR EXPERTS?   Roger A. Gold*
When choosing a doctor, lawyer, broker—*or any other expert*—how do you tell a knowledgeable man from an incompetent one This guide gives the answers!   AN0736—95

AWARD BOOKS, P.O. Box 500, Farmingdale, L.I., N.Y., 11735

Please send me the books indicated below by book number:

    SAVE $ $ $ 5 books or more, deduct 10% discount
    DISCOUNT 8 books or more, deduct 15% discount
    PLAN   10 books or more, deduct 20% discount

_____

_____

_____

If any of my selections are out of stock, please supply the following alternate choices. (List by book number):

_____

Name_____

Address_____

City_____State_____Zip_____

Add 25¢ for postage and handling for one book, 35¢ for two or three books. We pay postage on all orders of four books or more. Send remittance in U. S. or Canadian funds. Sorry, no C.O.D.'s.